LOVED CHILD
FOREVER TRASHED

CORA FLEETA HILL

NEWMAN SPRINGS PUBLISHING
320 Broad Street
Red Bank, NJ 07701

First originally published by Newman Springs Publishing 2023

ISBN 979-8-88763-458-6 (Paperback)
ISBN 979-8-88763-459-3 (Digital)

Printed in the United States of America

This book is dedicated to my adorable granddaughter Kya. Her very young life was neglected and snuffed out in a way unknown, and her tomb is unknown. Wherever her small fragile body was disposed, may my sweet darling granddaughter rest in peace. May God hold her in his tender arms now and forevermore.

PS: Perhaps one day, the truth shall be revealed as well as where she is. God's will be done.

If the city dump is where she lies, may "God's love and mercy carry her on the wings of angels into heaven.

I believe it's already done. Thank you, Lord Jesus.

To the Reader

This is a lamentation of the struggles involving the Department of Children and Family Services through the Common Pleas Court's Juvenile Court Division. This leads a family into the unseen tragedy of a young granddaughter. The guidance and judgments and legal decisions were not all in the child's best interest. It ultimately ended the young child's life. Her mother testified that she "put her in the trash."

Note from the Author

Reflections from the young child's agony: "Mother, stop. Mother, don't trash me! I am nobody's trash, so *no* bodies in the trash. No dumping allowed and no dumpster children. Hands off!"

The desire to write is to open up the need to radical changes in behavior. The deep heartfelt concern of child endangerment. Children illegally trashed through mama drama. The deadly outcome is not the end of this journey but only the beginning.

Many people play serious parts leading to the deadly end. People who are professional as well as nonprofessional. People who are guilty as well as innocent. People who are honest and the dishonest. People who are involved and not involved. People who are forgotten as well as the forgetful. People who are legal and the illegal. People who are young as well as the old. People who are loved and not loved. Finally, we need to protect the young from the old. Therefore, the names, locations, dates, and titles have been cleverly changed for all.

Book Arrangement

This book is naturally divided into three sections. It is divided by the paternal grandmother's journal entries. The second division is the paternal grandmother's emotional letters addressed to her missing young granddaughter. Her mother said she "put her in the trash."

The third section is the release of the public records from the legal court system. These legal documents were obtained from a concerned clerk of court upon the paternal grandmother's request.

The thirst for answers is now filled with empowerment. Including me, her paternal grandmother. I am to blame. I am guilty for losing my young granddaughter to being "caught up" in the system. *If only I knew what I know now!* Where's Kya? What happened?

The uncertainty actually stings, bringing deep burning aches, pumped-up heartbeats, and fierce mental exhaustion.

The body has not been found!

Preface

I was asleep at three in the morning when the phone woke me. It was a quiet unfamiliar voice on the other end. The young lady said she was calling from the hospital because she had been in an accident and was pregnant with my son's child (a little girl). That was a real eye-opener. However, after teaching second graders all week, I fell asleep! Wait. *Wait.* What just happened?

My son was incarcerated at the moment. So sad. The news was that my son was going to be a dad in two months! Kya's father is my "incarcerated son."

This book is written to also enlighten the awareness of grandparents to potential family situations that too often place our grandchildren in harm's way. The book is taken from a personal diary of the paternal grandmother. There are documented evidence and records obtained from the juvenile court system.

The Department of Children and Family Services was not truthful when first asked for information or records of Kya ever being in their care. The reply was there were no records. How could that be? Only of her siblings.

So not true. Kya's records were later obtained.

I personally took parenting classes at the facility in anticipation of the adoption of my grandbaby. What is the institution attempting to cover up? The lives of the silenced innocent little children.

The writer is Kya's paternal grandmother. The writing is surrounded in sincere duress, heartache, and hurt as well as the pain of guilt. These are strong emotions wrapped in lots of love.

March 19, 2022

Dear Journal,

Special crime scene unit TV show detectives find the remains of a five-to-six-year-old in a city trash compost. Should I watch the TV show or not? Decided to suffer through it. *Horrible* to relive the similar facts. The monstrous details of the murder of an innocent child… as my grandbaby happened to her. *Breathe deep. So hard to watch this.*

January 27, 2012

Life is good—background

Nana has five grandchildren. Two grandchildren belong to the daughter. Three grandchildren belong to the son. Nana loves her grandchildren dearly. She provides for them and even babysits on the weekends. Her home is the friendliest kids' place on the block. It consists of three bedrooms and one and one-half bathroom. Nana has become a single parent and manages somehow to balance out the monthly bills. It is not easy on a public school teacher's salary. She gives piano lessons. She is a Girl Scout leader at her school and goes camping too! *Life is good.*

I am the mother of two children, one of each (a boy and a girl).

Let's call the boy Josh and the girl Sue. Josh will bring headaches to me because he grows up to a future in prison (in and out, mostly in). However, he does become a father to a boy and two little darlings…the apples of my eyes, girls. Sue also has two beautiful and smart daughters. These grandchildren made up for the kinks in my life's chain of events, and life was good. One loving link was missing. What happened?

I continued my educational goal by traveling to Boston to receive a master's degree. This was a highlight in the grandmother's life.

Recent news!

March 19, 2022

Dear Journal,

So hard watching this crime scene investigation. This is *torture* again. I feel dirty, nasty, itchy…fainty. An innocent five-year-old murdered, raped, and tossed in the dumpster.

Child services placed-replaced by case worker. Child taken out of placement with little or no follow-up done. Too little too late. Where are the family records? Child missing for six weeks. No check on her. This case is so similar to mine!

The TV detectives go to the missing child's grandmother's house. The grandmother noted that a well-dressed white man came to her home from child services and took the little girl.

Someone took my precious baby too! Who? Perhaps this awareness will help to save other little girls (children). A series of tragic news reports. Devastating!

January 1, 2012

Dear Journal,

Happy New Year! I babysit two of my grandchildren. We go to church.

January 4, 2012

Dear Journal,

The phone call…my heart beats fast. My granddaughter Kya is in the custody of the court system. Kya's social worker is here. We filled out papers for me to appear in court by myself. Josh (her dad) incarcerated for three to six months. Unrelated case.

January 19, 2012

I visited my granddaughter at Children and Family Services. Kya is doing okay. Afterward, my second granddaughter and I went to church.

Visitations lasted three months or more.

January 21, 2012

Dear Journal,

Josh incarcerated. My son is in handcuffs from jail, and I go to Kya's trial. The child's mother, Dottie, was there also. Kya (the child) is okay. The mother refused to grant my request for child's last name change to ours. I was upset—definitely!

January 25, 2012

My graduation cap and gown came from graduate school. My phone was cut off. I forgot to pay it. Grandpa gave me a Christmas gift of $5,000. Wow! I gave one daughter-in-law $75 for her phone.

April 12, 2012

Dear Journal,

I am visiting Kya at the Foster and Adoptive care main campus building.

April 18, 2012

Dear Journal,

Grandmother is taking weekend classes to be able to *adopt* and care for her granddaughter who is presently in custody of the Children and Family Services. *I complete all the classes!*

I am also taking college teaching courses.

May 3, 2012

Kya is here visiting me!

May 16, 2012

Dear Journal,

Court date. The judge grants me (grandmother) guardianship of Kya! Time for transitioning the child from her foster care home to me.

May 21, 2012

Dear Journal,

Social worker calls. Kya is at urgent care emergency room.

May 22, 2012

Dear Journal,

I pick up Kya from Ms. Jones's house to spend the weekend with me!

May 29, 2012

Dear Journal,

I have guardianship of my granddaughter. Finally!

June 6, 2012

The social worker calls, and I am getting Kya Sunday at 5:00 p.m.

June 15, 2012

Grandmother picks up Kya at 5:00 p.m. from the foster care home.

June 16, 2012

We go to church.

June 23, 2012

Dear Journal,

We go to a restaurant.

June 29, 2012

Dear Journal,

Picked up Kya at 4:00 p.m. from foster care.

July 17, 2012

Dear Journal,

My house inspection for Kya.

July 19, 2012

I *adopted* my granddaughter Kya.

July 24, 2012

Dear Journal,

Kya is here.

July 25, 2012

Dear Journal,

Granny and I babysit!

August 3, 2012

Dear Journal,

We go to a restaurant and to the mall to shop.

August 4, 2012

Dear Journal,

Church.

August 5, 2012

Dear Journal,

Foster care mother calls me because Kya has a doctor checkup. We go to my brother's birthday party afterward.

August 10, 2012

Dear Journal,

A great day. My ex-husband (Kya's grandfather) took us to the county fair. Fun!

August 15, 2012

Dear Journal,

New baby bed, new toys. Great summer with my granddaughter Kya and other grandchildren. Free zoo on Mondays. We go to the zoo almost every Monday, except when I am teaching summer school.

August 16, 2012

Dear Journal,

Very busy summer but I love it! Kya and I go to the amusement park often. On weekends, we take a ferryboat ride across the lake to SeaWorld. Kya is in her umbrella stroller with our matching sun hats.

"Hi, Sue!" Her auntie (my daughter) works a roller-coaster ride at the park. So proud of my family!

August 17, 2012

Dear Journal,

Social worker meeting with Kya's mother and me.

December 1, 2012

Dear Journal,

Kya's mother comes to my house. Monitor visitations. Brings her boyfriend and his mother.

December 10, 2012

Kya's mother's supervised visitation at my home. Brings model children's kitchen set. Kya and her mom play together at my home.

December 26, 2012

Dear Journal,

I take Kya to her doctor for a checkup.

December 26, 2012

Dear Journal,

My granddaughter's pediatrician is so pleased with her progress while living with me. Kya loves her SpongeBob book pack. She is saying words now: "Ponge Bob" and "boo-boo." Kya laughs out loud as we go to the Chinese restaurant. I see the twinkle in my granddaughter's eyes as I pick her up from the longtime family babysitter. Hallelujah! Kya is walking. You can do it! She waddles like her dad (my son). I love her so much!

Merry Christmas
Very Happy New Year

While writing this book, I realize this is the moment of my true revelation. I now see that this is where I *should have* intervened. But I did not. As the grandparent, I should have said no to what followed.

Kya's mom gradually stepped in to remove my granddaughter from my home. *Stupid me.* I was too busy, wrapped up in the moment, to foresee the tragic future. *I failed* my granddaughter at this very moment in time. Too little, too late. I did not foresee her mother's ruthless intentions. Her mother was defying court orders.

February 1, 2013

Dear Journal,

My granddaughter's mom picks up the baby for a visit. I am teaching.

March 3, 2013

Dear Journal,

Kya goes to the babysitter Monday to Friday while I teach my class.

March 7, 2013

Dear Journal,

Kya's mom picks her up for the weekend.

March 12, 2013

Dear Journal,

Kya's mom calls, asks about Josh (the baby's father).

March 18, 2013

Dear Journal,

Kya is back.

March 28, 2013

Dear Journal,

We go for ice cream treats.

March 30, 2013

Dear Journal,

Kya's mom picks her up and takes toys and some clothes.

April 2, 2013

Dear Journal,

Social worker says I still have custody of her.

April 3, 2013

Kya and family go to Palm Sunday church. Her mom picks her up later.

April 4, 2013

Dear Journal,

My son is incarcerated at the moment. So sad. The news is my son is going to be a dad in one month. How sad but very true—to journal/write of a baby girl whose future is lost in this world or who cannot be found. The universe has consumed her. But where? What really happened to my young granddaughter? Will I ever know? (One person does know what really happened.)

Tell me. What's it all worth to you?

April 5, 2013

Dear Journal,

Some of the facts may come together to reveal answers to the empty-void space in my heart for my granddaughter. Kya's father is (named as) my "incarcerated son."

Letters to My Granddaughter Gone Too Soon
Grandma, Speak for Me
Two Broken Hearts, One Gone Forever

Dear Granddaughter Kya,

Grandma does not know if you still exist or not or what has really happened to you. (If I only knew.) The last time I saw you being taken away from my home was April 2013.

April 2013

Our two hearts were torn to pieces and our lives destroyed at the moment you were taken. You were terrified! Your face turned a pale color, then bright red blood was rushing to your pores. Grandma could see the fright in your twisted facial expression and hear you fall on the floor, kicking and hollering. Your piercing screams still resound. You did not want to go with your biological mother as she pulled you down my driveway and tossed you into her vehicle, leaving in her path two broken hearts.

(If only I knew.) I wish we could do a retake or a do-over. I would have held on to you so very tightly and never let you go! That was the last day. Savor it: that moment precious in time.

Love always for you (LAFY),
Grandma

Dear Granddaughter Kya,

Wake up, sweetie pie. This morning, we are having breakfast at Sunny's Fast Food before Nana goes to work. You like the pancakes from my "big breakfast" platter. I will carry my briefcase with the students' papers in it, and you carry your favorite bright yellow SpongeBob book bag. Your change of clothes and sippy cup are in it. Off to the babysitter! Can you say *SpongeBob*?

"Ponge Bob."

Good job, Kya. Let's go. Don't want to be late to Ms. Jones's house (babysitter)! Wish we could do this forever—be pals and stay together. Wish we could stay together forever. Car-seat time. Buckle up. (Both of us are laughing!)

Love always for you (LAFY),
Grandma

Dear Granddaughter Kya,

Grandma is on her way to pick you up. I am on my way to Ms. Jones's house (babysitter). School is out early today. My class is getting ready for open house this evening. I see you through the window in the walker to keep you safe.

"Hi, Kya. Grandma's here."

Look at that big, big smile. I am so happy too. I am a little tired from teaching and cleaning the second-grade classroom.

Hugs and open arms! Get your jacket and your SpongeBob book bag.

"Pong Pob."

Bye-bye! Got your diaper bag. Buckle up. Time to go home.

Love always for you (LAFY),
Grandma

Dear Granddaughter Kya,

Grandma is home. Parent conferences are over. Did you have fun with Great-Grandma? Wow! Twenty parents from my students showed up. What did you and my mom do? Patty cake, patty cake. Baker's man laughing. We're all smiles.

Grandmother talking with Kya

Let's eat ice cream tonight. Want some? Juice is in your sippy cup. Up the stairs to our bedroom. Tell my mom good night. Kya has a new day bed now right beside mine because she cried and screamed downstairs in her own bedroom. She must have felt *alone* or scared with the dim night light when she was by herself.

Say your prayers with me. Good night, Kya. Kya, luv ya. Oops! Don't forget to potty and training pants. Luv ya. Good night. Sleep tight.

Love always for you (LAFY),
Make today amazing!
Grandma

Dear Granddaughter Kya,

It's almost your birthday. You will be two years old next week. Say "two…two" (laughing). Now put up two fingers. One, two, buckle my shoe. Three, four, shut the door (laughing) song! We're singing "If You're Happy and You Know It, Clap Your Hands" and clapping.

Love always for you (LAFY),
Grandma

Dear Granddaughter Kya,

Come say hi to Great-Grandpa on the phone. We are taking him grocery shopping today. Your little cousin Mya is going also. She will stay with us today.

Get your SpongeBob book bag (diaper bag). Get into your car seat and buckle up. Mya too!

Hi, Great-Grandpa. We're at your house (phone). All are ready to go shopping. Kya loves bananas and chocolate pudding. Great-Grandpa had a great time! Clap-clap!

Love always for you (LAFY),
Grandma

Dear Granddaughter Kya,

Time for your checkup! Today, we go to your doctor. Say "doctor" (laughs) and "pediatrician." I am so excited and a little nervous. This is our first visit.

"Good morning doctor!"

Kya gets her checkup completed. The doctor is so very pleased with her progress. Her doctor comments on how happy she is. Kya is one year old, and her legs are getting stronger. She is standing! Kya is saying (baby) words. "Bye-bye," "Ponge Bob" (SpongeBob), and "bad butt" (her cousin says, laughing). She is also singing along to nursery rhymes. She was mute before. Grandma is so proud and happy for you!

Love always for you (LAFY),
Grandma

Dear Granddaughter Kya,

Well, you are starting to walk…taking steps. The doctor stood you up on his examining table. Grandma's big girl is one year old.

"Guess what? Chicken butt!" She loves rhyming words now. Is it time to take off the soft-bottom shoes? Let's go shopping for first-step walking shoes. We go to the outlet store to get properly fitted for Kya's first pair of shoes. They are white lace hard-bottoms! It's time!

Love always for you (LAFY),
Grandma

Dear Granddaughter Kya,

Today is Great-Grandpa's birthday. It's a surprise party at Auntie Sue's house. Let's go. Get your SpongeBob diaper bag. We are picking up Great-Grandpa at his house.

Surprise! See, your cousins and family are here. Run, play, and have fun.

Kya goes downstairs. I take her downstairs with all the children and teens too. Yeah! Pizza, chicken, ice cream, chips, and cake. Help Great-Grandpa blow out ninety candles and sing "Happy Birthday"!

Bye-bye Let's go home!

Love always for you (LAFY),
Grandma

Dear Granddaughter Kya,

Wake up! Grandpa is taking us and your little cousin Mya to the Ohio state fair. Rise and shine! Grandpa is here. Get your SpongeBob book bag and our new sun caps. What a beautiful day! Buckle up!

We are at the fair. "Yes, you may pet the little lambs." I laugh.

Next, we all ride the merry-go-round two times. Hold on. Now wash your hands for the cotton candy and yummy french fries!

The fun fair day is over. Bye-bye, Grandpa. Thanks. Thank you! *Love you!*

Love always for you (LAFY),
Grandma

Dear Granddaughter Kya,

Grandma is home from teaching summer school to all the second-grade kids. Let's call our neighbor—your big friend Lea—to go out to eat at her favorite spot. (Lea is thirteen years old, and she is also in the custody of relatives: her aunt.) Let's go. Don't forget SpongeBob (diaper bag).

"Hi, Lea!"

We go to the Chinese Buffet Restaurant. Kya eats and laughs with Lea. Such a wonderful time! All done! Let's go home!

Love always for you (LAFY),
Grandma

Dear Granddaughter Kya,

Good morning, Kya. Today is Halloween. Your cousins are coming today. We all are going to trick or treat. ("Tick tee.") Let's get a costume for you. Get your book bag ("Bong Bop") SpongeBob diaper bag. Buckle up!

Do you like this pumpkin costume? Next, we go to the store to buy a real pumpkin to carve. Kya, your cousins are here.

We put the pumpkin in the middle of the table. I cut out the top and bake the seeds.

Now draw a face on the pumpkin. Make a mouth, a nose, and two big eyes. Put a light inside the pumpkin. Halloween surprise! (Singing and clapping.)

Love always for you (LAFY),
Grandma

Dear Granddaughter Kya,

Your mom is visiting today. Your mom is coming here to play with you. She is bringing a gift for you. Grandma will be here also.

Kya, your mom is here. Hello. Hi. We will put the toy kitchen together. Your mom brought this for you.

Did you have fun today with your mom? Tell Mom bye-bye. "If You're Happy and You Know It, Clap Your Hands" (*clap clap*). Let's say our prayers. Good night!

Love always for you (LAFY),
Grandma

Dear Granddaughter Kya,

It's your birthday! Two years old. Aunty Sue is having a birthday party for you. Yeah! Let's get dressed to go to her apartment. Grandma is so proud of you because you are walking. Your cousins will be at your party.

Time for your birthday party. Let's go. Buckle up. Yes! We got SpongeBob (diaper bag).

Happy birthday to you…cha cha cha.

Love always for you (LAFY),
Grandma

Dear Journal,

Kya has lived with me for two years, ten months, and nineteen days. Kya's mother has visitations. I meet her boyfriend because he drives her sometimes. Kya does not act comfortable around her mother. Her eyes are shifty-looking, and her facial expressions look tense. I am near to reassure her she is safe and in a safe and loving space. The social worker calls to check to see if the visitations are "okay."

March 21, 2022

Present time

The missing links are finally coming together exactly twenty years later. Kya would be turning twenty-one years old.

After extensively researching into official court records for the reason for the child's removal from my custody home. Finally, all these years of guilt and blame of not following up and keeping my baby are exonerated. The stomach pains and heavy eyes can be loosed.

I was not the reason Kya was returned to her mom.

Where is she?

What happened?

Why?

March 21, 2022

Present time, legal matters

On July 14, 2013, this case came up for consideration before an administrative hearing officer of the Support Enforcement Agency that one or more parties failed to submit themselves for the genetic testing as required by Ohio law. The hearing officer further finds that it is inconclusive as to whether the alleged father is the natural father of Kya. It is *therefore ordered* that no orders establishing the existence or nonexistence of the parent-child relationship between Josh and Kya be issued at this time.

March 21, 2022

Enclosed is also a copy of the following document pertaining to the administrative paternity case. This letter was sent to Josh. The paternity case *x*. Dismissal order. My son was dismissed from the paternity case. Not true. He was tested.

February 21, 2022

My granddaughter Ann found the whereabouts of Kya's mom. Ann is thinking that Kya is her missing sister. She is very upset and has been angry about what could have happened to her. Kya's mom is discovered working in a store. She will soon visit her.

The two girls are both my granddaughters but have two different mothers. Ann, the one granddaughter, says she remembers her stepsister Kya. Ann is angry because her stepsister was "put in the trash." Ann goes to Kya's insane mother to find answers.

Where is her stepsister?

What happened to her stepsister?

Why?

Still no closure. Still no body.

Heart-wrenching.

Now my back aches so badly, I will take a break from writing!

PS: Ann reminds me so much of Kya. Indeed, sisters bond!

Public Records——Court Procedure

Reasonable efforts were made by the Department of Children and Family Services to prevent the removal of the child from the home, and removal is in the best interest of the child.

The social worker, Department of Children and Family Services first being duly sworn, that a child in *dependency* as defined in Section 2151.04 (D) of the Revised Code in the following particulars:

1. Mother has had siblings of the child removed in the past due to mother's chronic and severe mental issues (Case #).
2. Mother has had a psychological evaluation done by the juvenile court clinic in the past wherein she was diagnosed with antisocial personality disorder and depression, and the clinic recommended she not receive custody of a sibling of the child, either now or in the future.
3. Mother's mental health issues severely limit mother's written in *interfere* with her ability to provide a safe and stable home for the child either now or in the foreseeable future.
4. Mother has also been diagnosed with depression, which prevents her from providing adequate care for the child.
5. Mother has a history with CCDCFS due to issues of neglect. Mother left a sibling of the child home alone in deplorable living conditions.
6. Mother was charged with child endangerment.
7. A sibling of the child is in the legal custody of his father.
8. Mother has failed to remedy the conditions, causing the child to be placed outside the home.

9. Alleged father of the child has not established paternity and provides no care or support for the child. His whereabouts are unknown.
10. Alleged father was convicted of attempted drug trafficking.
11. The child is at an age to most benefit from a permanent home, which cannot be achieved without a grant of permanent custody to CCDCFS.

Reasonable efforts were made by County Department of Children and Family Services to prevent the removal of the child from the home, and removal is in the best interest of the child. The child was removed March/April pursuant to Ohio Revised Code Sections 5153.16 (A) (7) and 2151.31 (A) (3).

Wherefore, the undersigned prays this honorable court grants a disposition of *permanent custody* to CCDCFS: grant an order of support on the parents of the child, including maintenance of any medical, surgical, or hospital policies of insurance for the child that existed at the time of filing this complaint or an order to obtain health insurance coverage for the child; and to make such further orders as the court deems just and proper.

Loved
Child
Forever
Trashed

The paternal grandmother loved the child.
Kya's memory will last forever. She is forever in my heart.
The child's deranged mother said she put her child in the trash.

Dear Journal,

Now comes the state of County Child Support Enforcement Agency, Juvenile Division here in after "CSEA" by the through the County Prosecutor, and his undersigned assistant pursuant to Rule 19 of the Rules of Civil Procedure.

Further, CSEA states that the mother and child are both residents of the county; that the mother gave birth to the minor child; Josh is the father of the minor child: that no other male is presumed to be the father of said child. Josh will establish paternity of Kya and provide necessary support for her care.

Josh had to appear in court in March. However, he is imprisoned in the county jail. It was a court order pursuant to Revised Code Section 2317.06, that the county sheriff's office transport party from said institution to this court for hearing on the date indicated on the attached summons/subpoena and to return him to said institution after his presence is no longer needed by the court. This transport order was filed with the clerk and journalized.

This matter came on for hearing before the assigned judge (judge by assignment) upon a complaint for dependency and prayer for permanent custody.

The assistant county prosecutor entered an oral motion for a genetic test to be performed. The court, after due consideration, grants the oral motion.

It is therefore ordered that the mother, her child, and the alleged father shall appear at the County Child Support Enforcement Agency and be interviewed and subsequently submit themselves for genetic testing to GeneScreen, a duly qualified examiner approved by the court, at such time and place as directed by the Support Enforcement Agency.

It is therefore ordered that the previous Order of Emergency Temporary custody to the County Department of Children and Family Services is continued in effect.

It is *further ordered* that this cause be and hereby is continued May 10, for Genetic Testing to be completed and for trial.

GeneScreen uses DNA testing exclusively for paternity tests. The primary type of testing utilizes a technique called polymerase chain reaction. Polymerase chain reaction (PCR) is a technique used to make many copies of specific sections of an individual's DNA. These sections are passed from parents to children. One person's DNA differs from another's by the length of these specific sections. The lengths are expressed as numbers (like 5.0 or 11.0). Everyone has two numbers in each genetic system. If a number is only shown once (like 5.0), it means that both numbers are the same (5.0, 5.0). A child always inherits one number from its mother and one from its biological father.

Paternity testing is based on a simple principle of biology: children inherit genetic factors from both biological parents, with each parent passing on half of a child's genetic factors. If he does possess all the genetic factors, he is *included*, and a probability is calculated that he is the father. A probability of paternity of 99 percent or greater indicates a strong likelihood that the alleged father is the biological father of the child.

The alleged father shall be tested. He will establish paternity in prison, at the Federal Correctional Institution.

The mother and the child shall submit themselves for genetic testing to GeneScreen, a duly qualified expert approved by the court. The fee for the tests will be paid by the County Child Support Enforcement Agency (CSEA).

Probability of Paternity: 99.97 Percent

This is accredited by the American Association of Blood Banks for paternity testing utilizing DNA analysis. My son has established paternity of my granddaughter. Hallelujah!

Josh is the father of the minor child, that *no other male* is presumed to be the father of said child, and that CSEA has assumed the responsibility of collection of support. CSEA further requests that for this court order, the father pay the birthing expenses of the minor child, a reasonable amount for the past, current, and future support for the minor child, including health insurance. And it further orders that the father reimburse assistance provided for the minor child and, finally, that the court grant all equitable relief to which the parties are entitled.

Dear Journal,

I must pause here, taking a plug in the springtime air freshener! Mental health break, looking at a beautiful spring picture magazine. The morning is used up, and now to enjoy the beautiful blossoming trees and flowers. Also, observation of the squirrels, birds, and, oh. I see deer. So carefree.

Praying that my intense chest pains will go away. My shoulders are also sore because I am overwhelmed with sorrow.

Dear Journal,

Stopped writing this book for three weeks. Suffered heart failure. I went to a new cardiologist. Relaxed a bit. Bad chest pains for two weeks.

Now it is necessary for me to organize my new writing area. It is sanitized, decluttered, and aroma fresh. The birds can be heard singing.

This child-abuse reality must continue to be addressed. The book must be completed regardless.

It has been determined by the court that my son is the father 99 percent. He was tested in the federal prison. The procedures are legal. This is my grandbaby. My love for Kya is genuine. Her father is still incarcerated.

He calls his mother (me) approximately ten to fifteen times daily from the prison. Ridiculous! Stress up!

Now comes the State of Ohio. A letter was sent to my son, addressed to the county jail.

The summons was filed as a Case Class: EMR emergency and Case Type Abuse, Dependency, Neglect.

You are hereby commanded to appear for a trial hearing before this court. This matter will be heard by Judge custody 5p.

1. You and/or your child have the right to be represented by a lawyer at all stages of the proceedings, or the rights to a lawyer may be waived. If you wish to be represented by a lawyer but are financially unable to employ one, you have the right to have a lawyer provided for you. Therefore, if you wish to have a lawyer but believe that you cannot afford one, contact the Public Defender office at (000-000).

2. Pursuant to Rule 10 (C) and Rule 44 (B) of the state Rules of Criminal Procedure, you have the right to retain counsel even if you intend to plead guilty, and you have the right to a reasonable continuance in the proceedings to secure counsel, and the right to have counsel assigned without cost, if indigent.

3. The complaint, motion, or application requests on order of permanent custody. If the court grants permanent custody of the child, the parents and other relatives will lose forever all parental rights and privileges, including the right to decide where the child will live, what religion he will

receive, what his name shall be, and whether he will be adopted. Also, all duties, including the obligation to support and provide care for the child, will forever end.

4. Witness must report to the clerk in the court room for which they are subpoenaed in order to ensure the taxation of their fees

5. A Parent-Child Relationship Complaint has been filed in this court. You have the right to admit or deny the allegations contained in the attached complaint. You have the right to trial by jury by filing a demand within three days after the action is set for trial.

6. A motion violation has been filed in this court. You have the right to have an attorney represent you.

   If the motion is entitled "Motion to Show Cause" or "Violation of Court Order," you are hereby notified that your failure to appear, in response to the attached summons, may result in the court issuing an order for your arrest and also order that any support ordered be withheld from your personal earnings or other income source you may have.

A neglected child, as defined in RC 2151.03 (A), includes any child

1. who is abandoned by the child's parents, guardian, or custodian.

2. who lacks adequate parental care because of the faults or habits of the child's parents, guardian, or custodian.

3. whose parents, guardian, or custodian neglects the child or refuses to provide proper or necessary subsistence, education, medical or surgical care or treatment, or other care necessary for his health, morals, or well-being.

4. whose parents, guardian, or custodian neglects the child or refuses to provide the special care made necessary by the child's mental condition.

5. who, because of the omission of the child's parents, guard-
    ian, or custodian, suffers physical or mental injury that
    harms or threatens to harm the child's health or welfare.
6. who is subjected to out-of-home care child neglect.

An abused child, as defined in RC 2151.031, is any child who

1. is the victim of "sexual activity" as defined under RC 2907,
    where such activity would constitute an offense under that
    chapter, except that the court need not find that any person
    has been convicted of the offense in order to find that the
    child is an abused child.
2. exhibits evidence of any physical or mental injury or death,
    inflicted other than by accidental means, or an abused
    child injury or death that is at variance with the history
    given of it.
3. because of the acts of his parents, guardian, or custodian,
    suffers physical or mental injury that harms or threatens to
    harm the child's health or welfare.
4. is subjected to out-of-home care child abuse.

Kya was not placed in "Permanent Custody," which means an order of a juvenile court pursuant to which both of the following apply: (a) legal custody of a child is given to a public children services agency or private child placing agency, all parental rights duties, and obligations, including the right to consent to adoption, and divests the natural parents or adoptive parents of all parental rights.

Kya was placed in "Planned Permanent Living Arrangement," which means an order of a juvenile court pursuant to which both of the following apply:

a. Legal custody of a child is given to a public children ser-
    vices agency or a private child placing agency *without* the
    terminator of parental rights.
b. The agency is permitted to make appropriate placement of
    the child and to enter into a written agreement with a fos-

ter care provider or with any other person or agency with whom the child is placed.

The case plans of the mother's older children were identified. The older children were in the custody of their fathers.

Now it is time for Kya's action case plans to be put into place. The first need, priority number one, is emotional stability. The referral is made to the family clinic. Kya's concern isolating herself from her mother and siblings.

The second need of the action plan concern is employment.

The third need of the action plan is paternity. Josh has established paternity. It is unsure if he maintains contact or provides support.

The fourth need of services is domestic relations and family violence. This need specifically applied to only Josh. Why? Both parents were in great need of this violence intervention. This intervention may have saved my granddaughter the tragic ending. This was so sadly overlooked by the agency, the most important individual threat and concern.

The detailed need description is stated in the case plan. What is the number one need/concern? The concern is the parenting skills for the mother and father:

1. What behavior will change this concern to reduce risk and address safety issues of the child?

    The mother and father will actively participate in and demonstrate appropriate parenting skills verified by a parenting certificate.

    The goals and needs are very well stated. However, these are wishful thinking unless each one is strictly enforced by professionals and individually monitored on a consistent basis. Understandable that the basic needs of the child are met and safety are the number one priority. However, do not underestimate the power of a parent to manipulate and twist the system. The parent, for whatever private reasons, may selfishly want to keep the child.

The parent does whatever is necessary but fails to control the behaviors. Therefore, the goals may be unattainable (impossible to attain).

2. What specific activities do family members need to do to make this change (build on family strength here)?

Mother and father will attend parenting classes. Mother and father will comply with rules of program and recommendations. Ultimately not measurable. Mother and father will actively participate in parenting classes.

3. How will the social worker and/or service team help the family make this change?

SW (social worker) will provide parents with parenting referrals. SW will provide case management and ongoing services.

4. How and when will the family's progress be measured?

Progress will be measured by home visits, phone contacts, and provider reports.

5. How and when will the family's progress be reviewed?

Progress will be reviewed by staffing.

The next action plan need/concern is employment and self-sufficiency:

1. Mother will attain stable full-time employment verified by pay stubs.

2. Mother will check newspapers and job boards for employment. Mother will go on interviews for employment. Mother will participate in a job training program to enhance job skills.

3. The social worker will make suggestions for possible job opportunities. The SW (social worker) will refer the mother to job training. The SW will provide case management and ongoing services.

4. Progress will be measured by reports, phone contacts, and home visits.

5. The family's progress will be reviewed by staffings.

The action plan need/concern is substance abuse:

1. What behavior will change this concern to reduce risk and address safety issues of the child?

    Mother and father will maintain and provide a drug-free environment for their child. Mother and father will complete a drug assessment and comply with all random urine screens.
2. What specific activities do family members need to do to make this change (build on family strength here)?

    Mother and father will come to CCDCFS for a drug assessment on the scheduled day. Mother and father will complete assessment and comply with all recommendations. Mother and father will go to random urine screens on day designated by SW.
3. How will the social worker and/or service team help the family make this change?

    SW will assist parents during assessment. SW will provide referral for assessment. SW will inform parents of time and day of random urine screens. SW (Social worker) will provide case management.
4. How and when will the family's progress be measured?

    Progress will be measured through provider reports, phone contacts, and home visits.
5. How and when will the family's progress be reviewed?

    Progress will be reviewed by staffings.

The next action plan need/concern is the child's characteristics. The detailed need is the child is waking up in the middle of the night, screaming.

1. What behavior will change this concern to reduce risk and address safety issues of the child?

    The child will be able to sleep through the night without waking up screaming. This will be addressed through child therapy.

2. What specific activities do family members need to do to make this change (build on family strength here)?

Foster parents will take the child to all appointments and follow recommendations.

3. How will the social worker and/or service team help the family make this change?

SW (social worker) will make referral for counseling with resource department. SW will provide case management. SW will refer to all necessary services.

4. How and when will the family's progress be measured?

Progress will be measured through provider reports, phone contacts, and office and home visits.

5. How and when will the family's progress be reviewed?

Progress will be reviewed by staffings.

The father, Josh, has a history of domestic violence and in need of entering a domestic violence perpetrator program.

1. What behavior will change this concern to reduce risk and address safety issues of the child(ren)?

Father will successfully complete a domestic violence program.

2. What specific activities do family members need to do to make this change (build on family strength)?

Father will schedule his intake appointment for the DV program. Father will attend all sessions and actively participate in all his sessions. Father will be able to demonstrate his new knowledge and skills.

3. How will the social worker and/or service team help the family make this change?

The social worker will refer the father to domestic violence programs. SW will provide case management.

4. How and when will the family's progress be measured?

Progress will be measured by provider reports and phone contacts.

5.   How and when will the family's progress be reviewed?
        Family's progress will be reviewed every six months at
the semiannual review.

It is negligent for a six-month family review. The concern needs
to be addressed monthly. Family progress should be *closely* monitored!
    This life drama *now* takes two turns *at the same time*. One turn
is in the rewarding direction, but the other turn is very tragic. My
family is ecstatic because there is a hearing scheduled to allow Kya to
live with me. The hearing is to grant custody to the paternal grandmother (*me*). Her dad is incarcerated at this time. The grandmother
and great-grandmother live in the home. The home has three bedrooms, living room, dining room, sunporch, and one and a half
baths. It is described as a bungalow.
    The home is located in a suburb very close to the city. It has
an exceptionally large backyard and a two-car detached garage. It is
very close to the vicinity where Kya's mother "says" she lives. We live
approximately only two miles apart. They live in the inner city. The
school in which I teach second grade is in walking distance to Kya's
house!
    Note: This is how close our lives are entwined with one another.
How ironic is that!
    Please, *please* just bring her to me!

There is a hearing in November. The permanency effort document reads that the PGM (paternal grandmother) is interested in
having Kya placed with her, now that paternity has been established.
Present at the hearing Tuesday, at 1:30 p.m., were the assigned counsel, guardian ad litem, father, and mother. Results of the preliminary
hearing are continued for pretrial Thursday at 1:30 p.m. The hearing
notice was issued and sent by way of personal service.
    The Document Permanency Efforts section 9 asks the question
if any child was with a goal of adoption or planned permanent living
arrangement. Neither box (yes or no) is checked. Red flag!
    However, the court determined that Kya's visits with the pater-
nal grandmother (PGM) will start next week. The social worker at

the specific recruitment agency explained the difference between an adoptive home or other permanent home. It is noted that the PGM is still considered as to whether she wants to adopt or have permanent custody. A follow-up by staffing was scheduled. *The paternal grandmother decided to adopt.* Follow-up meeting not needed.

Dear Journal,

I am teaching and family oriented during the week. However, the weekends for eight weeks are spent in classes at the Children and Family Services building. So proud. My parenting diploma is displayed in the dining room at my house. The scheduled follow-up staffing was cancelled. Kya will be placed in the home of the PGM.

Kya will start visiting the PGM next week. However, before the home visits, Great-Grandpa comes also to the Children and Family Services building to help get acquainted with our new little family member. We also met her big brother and maternal grandmother. One big *very happy* family. We visit and bond together for six weeks. Maternal grandmother stated that she took care of Kya as a newborn but, unfortunately, had to give her up. She and the mother's boyfriend had called for services. The signatures included the social worker, the maternal grandmother, the other panel member, the facilitator, and myself.

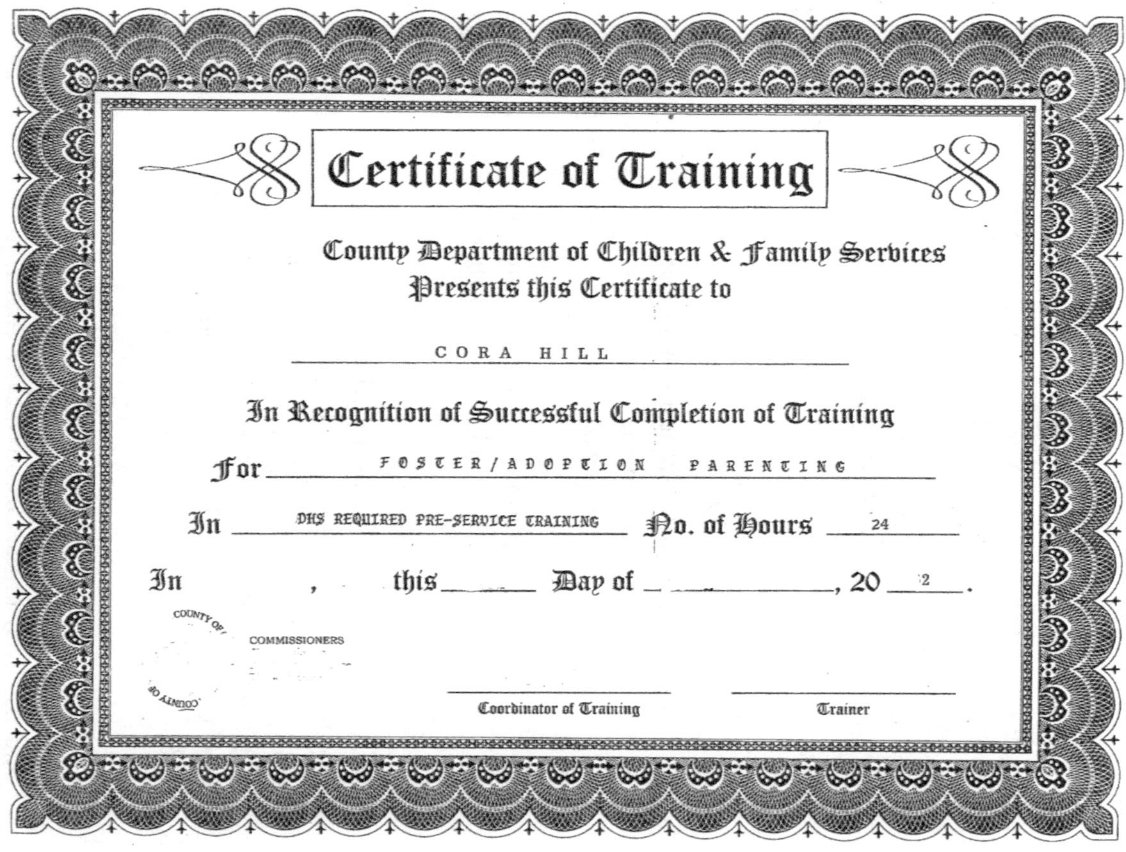
Certificate of Training
County Department of Children & Family Services
Presents this Certificate to
CORA HILL
In Recognition of Successful Completion of Training
For   FOSTER/ADOPTION   PARENTING
In   DHS REQUIRED PRE-SERVICE TRAINING   No. of Hours   24
In   ,   this   Day of   , 20   2 .
COUNTY OF
COMMISSIONERS
COUNTY OF
Coordinator of Training
Trainer

Court procedure

This matter is set for trial hearing at 9:00 a.m. The results of the trial hearing request of county prosecutor. The child herein is placed with the paternal grandmother during the pendency of this cause. Present at the hearing are the father's attorney, the social worker, the mother, the attorney, and the paternal grandmother.

The case plan (CP) is documented as follows:

a. Kya—Type of placement
b. Certified/approved relative
c. Date placed
d. Restricted visitation
e. Supervised visitation
f. Who may visit? Mother (name)
g. Where (location)? Grandmother's home
h. How often (frequency)? Two times a week and will be increased every couple of weeks *until child is reunified.* This was *not* told to me.
i. How long (duration)? Overnight and day visits. (What? Overnight visits with child and mother were *not* discussed with me.)

Very controversial to the original review of Structured Decision Making (SDM) results wherein it is written that reunification is not the goal (twice).

Kya's date of birth is March 4, ——. It is recorded with the Court of Common Pleas Juvenile Division the child was removed March 6, ——. The same year, only two days old.

Dear Journal,

Kya has been in the custody of the courts and in foster care for eight months. The previous order of emergency temporary custody to the County Department of Children and Family Services is continued in effect. The foster care home also wanted to adopt Kya. This would eliminate all family connections to the child. I was desperate for this not to happen. Little did I know that the foster home adoption would have been the *safest* decision for my granddaughter. Hindsight not there!

Court procedure

There is much preparation. The social worker interviews me at my house. The checklist of items that must be approved is extensive. I have placed the necessary paperwork and documents in a three-ring binder on the living room table. The checklist includes the following:

1. social security card
2. job paycheck stubs
3. mortgage statement
4. proof of residency
5. health issues
6. religious preference
7. pets
8. driver's license
9. health insurance lasts months
10. utility bills—phone, gas, light, water
11. divorce papers
12. drug/alcohol use
13. household members

The Foster Parent Checklist also includes the items below:

1. proof of auto liability insurance
2. background checks for alternate
3. caregivers and all adults living in the home
4. welfare fraud repayment verification or plan
5. complete medical forms, filled out by physician (within 180 days prior to license)
6. evacuation plan
7. financial statement
8. picture of current family members

9. proof of residency (last five years from date of fingerprinting)
10. reference from boss of job experience

After the completion of the Foster Parent Checklist, the social worker does a walkthrough of the home. She checks for safety issues (paint, lead, etc.). The social worker (SW) also notes the living arrangements of the residents. "Where will Kya sleep?" The child must have *her own bedroom and bed* (crib). The electrical outlets are covered with safety caps. There are night-lights in her room. The room also has spacious windows to let the sunshine in. Kya has a spacious backyard to play in with a birdbath.

Our home has plenty of room in my life for my little granddaughter. Thank you, Lord!

My final medical form has one side to be completed by a licensed physician. The more direct medical questions include the following:

- Have you had treatment for a serious or chronic illness?
- Have you been hospitalized in the past five years?
- Have you ever received, or been advised to seek, mental health services?
- Have you ever received treatment for alcohol or substance abuse?

The answers to the medical questions were completed with "no". Another form is completed!

The hearing has been set for March 7. Warning: Failure to attend this hearing may result in the loss of temporary or permanent custody of the child in this matter or the issuance of a contempt citation or arrest order.

Kya's mother, father, paternal grandmother (me), lawyers, social worker—we all stood before the visiting judge in Courtroom A.

Kya is placed in emergency custody (EC) with her paternal grandmother. This is not an out-of-state placement. The child is placed within five miles of the mother's home.

There are four family team meeting reports. The goals are to discuss visitation rules, dates, times, and location. The team will plan case objectives and discuss the child's permanency.

The visits will be held inside the paternal grandmother's home every other Thursday from 5:30 to 7:30 p.m. and supervised. All parties sign this attachment.

Please report any problems or concerns the paternal grandmother may have regarding the visits in her home.

It is therefore ordered that the child Kya be and hereby is placed with the paternal grandmother until further orders of the court.

It is therefore ordered that the previous Order of Emergency Temporary Custody to the County Department of Children and Family Services is continued in effect. Signed by the judge and deputy clerk.

The next step in the process is that Kya visits with the paternal grandmother. She visits on the weekends for three weeks. The social services van driver brings her. I see her in the driveway. He toots the horn. Kya is peeking out from inside her car seat and smiling. I go outside to welcome my granddaughter into her new loving family. My prayers have been answered.

Dear Granddaughter Kya,

We will be together every day. You are my special little girl. Let's put your pretty things in this SpongeBob book bag. (I clap. Kya claps.) We will take them with us. Don't forget the small picture frame of "Mary Had a Little Lamb." You can carry it. This is our car and your car seat. Buckle up. We are going home together.

Love always for you (LAFY),
Grandma

Dear Granddaughter Kya,

Hello. Great-Grandmother is here. She loves you too—very, very much. Let's get a little hug, show some love. (We all laugh.)

Kya, this is your new room. You have a new bed, your clothes, and look—toys! The ones you brought with you are pretty also. You are special. Your things are special.

Just come sit on the floor next to Grandma. This is a busy-bee day (*buzz*). Let's clap and sing "If You're Happy and You Know It."

"If you're happy and you know it, clap your hands—*clap clap*. Stamp your feet and say amen."

I love the Lord.

Love always for you (LAFY),
Grandma

Now the true bonding begins. Realizing this is a new family for all of us. The house has a different "air" about it. Kya is surrounded by support and compassion. My schedule is very busy but *totally rewarding*.

The Critical Issues/Services for Custody Cases reviews the placement. This review team has determined that the child's current placement is safe and appropriate.

Kya has been receiving all her needs in the home of the paternal grandmother since 07-24. Kya is up-to-date with all exams with no medical concerns at this time. This is determined by the case management team. The child is in the least restrictive setting. The kinship investigation is completed. My "incarcerated son" is Kya's father. The paternal grandmother will meet all the child's basic needs. The child's basic needs and *safety is being met*.

Must stop writing because I'm experiencing shoulder pain, aches, and leg cramps. The pressure mentally as well as physically is overwhelming. Take a quiet outdoors walk. Walk the puppy! *Praise the Lord!*

The reality of child abuse must continue to be addressed. The book must be completed regardless.

Child Loved
Forever Trashed
Represented with Venn Diagram

Child Loved
Forever Trashed

Dear Journal,

I am nervous and excited. Today, Kya is going to her doctor's checkup appointment. The agency mailed her medical card in a large manila envelope along with a personal journal to keep records and pictures in.

"Buckle up. Away we go." It is time for Kya's ten-months-old pediatrics examination. She is lifted onto the exam table straight face. Kya seems to remember her doctor. Kya says hi! The doctor completes the exam.

Kya says "bye-bye," waves, and mumbles other sounds (like singing). The doctor is surprised and so very pleased at the progress being made. He says Kya made no response in the past. Now she is learning communication skills. Says "knee" when tapped. Says "eye." What a great improvement altogether!

A very rewarding doctor's checkup.

Dear Kya,

"Kya, take your lollipop and say 'thank you.' If you're happy and you know it, clap your hands."

She says "clap-clap."

Buckle up. It's another busy day. What a smart girl. I will open the lollipop treat for you. The ride home takes a long time. Grandmother is very happy and proud of you. Let's go home.

Love always for you (LAFY),
Grandma

Dear Granddaughter Kya,

Your face is not a happy one. You are little, and Grandmother is big. You are new, and Grandmother is old. I love you. Here's a little hug. Come sit in our rocking chair and hold a little book. I will hold you until your eyes shut. Oh, don't cry. Wipe your eyes. Go to sleep, little baby. Rock, rock, rock in our rocking chair and rock, rock, rock some more!

Love always for you (LAFY),
Grandma

Dear Journal,

Kya lived with me for two years, ten months, and nineteen days. Kya's mother has visitations. I meet her "boyfriend" because he drives her sometimes. Kya does not act comfortable around her mother. Her eyes are shifty-looking, and her facial expressions look awfully tense.

I am near to reassure Kya that she is still safe and in a loving space. The social worker calls every week to see if the visitations are okay.

Dear Journal,

My mind is in turmoil. The social worker calls. She tells me Kya's mother had a court hearing granted for overnights at her home with the child. There is a *motion to terminate protective supervision*. The Department of Children and Family Services, by and through counsel, respectfully moves this court for an order terminating protective supervision of Kya and vesting legal custody of the child in the mother *with no restrictions*.

Moreover, it states that the granting of this motion is in the child's best interest, as is more fully explained in the brief in support. This document was signed by a different social worker and the county prosecuting attorney.

Kya's placement is overnight and day visits at her mother's home. The frequency (two times per week) will be increased every couple of weeks until the child is reunited. The mother has completed her case plan successfully. Last psychological recommends reunification. Mother's cooperative efforts with Children and Family Services has *reduced the risk* to the child so as to allow them to remain in the home. *Noted paternal grandmother is not notified of the motion being filed nor granted.*

The previous Detailed Need description notes plainly the mother's mental health is a concern due to the lack of concern regarding her children's health, safety, and well-being. Earlier, the results of the review of Structured Decision Making states, "Reunification is not the goal."

The number one need is emotional stability. The recommendations by the —— (name white out) clinic were for family reunification. Initially, the provider was concerned that Kya was isolating herself from her mother and sibling. "They worked with her, and she has become more sociable and involved with the family."

The report also recommended that the mother work on improving *self-esteem. However, the mother does not believe she needs to improve her self-esteem.* (A red flag.) The social worker has observed the mother to be very motivated and cooperative. The mother is employed full-time and is managing her money well. Mother has successfully completed services to a moderate level (checked box). The Safety Reassessment safety decision box is checked (x) safe. Included Substance Abuse progress response.

Dear Journal,

Kya's mother participates in the case plan management program. She apparently completes the program using a private firm. The positive results are then handed over papers to the courts. The new documents are processed and approved for reunification of the child with her mother (*tragic mistake*). Red flag. The paternal grandmother is unaware of these new documents!

Recent news

It has been reported that there was a police raid on an unknown house, a suspected meth lab. The police have been called out twelve times.

Witnesses say that Children and Family Services does wellness checks only on the two children. The concern being how could the department miss the fact that the children are not dressed and not fed. The house caught fire and blew up. Three children were rescued to foster homes. Finally, the neighbors were very disturbed at the neglect and reports ignored that were made.

More recent news

A mother is presently on trial for throwing her baby boy in the trash around twenty years ago. The DNA samples caught up with her. The question is was he alive or dead when he was discarded? The questions perhaps were not honestly answered. Authorities state the bones were found as remains in a field, and animals had gnawed on him. "No dumping allowed" of our precious babies.

Dear Journal,

Stopped writing this book for three weeks. Suffered heart failure. Went to a new cardiologist (my doctor retired). Relaxed a bit; chest pains for two weeks. Prayers. Praise the Lord.

Dear Journal,

My mind is in turmoil. The social worker says she is getting married and moving out of state (sounded very happy). She tells me to pack up all Kya's belongings. Her mother is on her way to pick her up. *What? Why?*

The social worker stated that the mother had completed all her intervention programs and was being immediately reunited with her child. This shocked me. Total shock and desperation. Unfathomable, unreal, unexpected, and unnecessary.

I should have said it was unacceptable but instead ignorantly complied with the court order. It is downhill shot to hell from now on. Kya is returned to her "mother."

Dear Journal,

The family is taking a family portrait because there are four generations living. I call Kya's mother to pick her up one week in advance. We all so much love for my granddaughter to be in the family picture with "the girls."

We are wearing gold shirts and black bottoms. I have Kya's out-fit ready. There is not a problem picking her up on Saturday. Kya's mother finally answers the phone and says that she will bring her. She can come! Happy are we! She will give us her address. *It never happened.*

Grandpa and I go to the addresses listed with Children and Family Services. Abandoned homes. More lies and more lies.

No communication. No granddaughter. Mother's discretion, *not mine.* Tragic.

Lord, help me. Lord, please keep my granddaughter safe. Wrap her in your lovin' arms.

This reality of child abuse must continue to be addressed. The book must be completed regardless! *Regardless!*

More Recent News! The three-year-old boy in child protective custody was living with the court-appointed family. The mother was found neglecting the child care. The results going through the court system is to keep the child out of harm's way! The foster care family has the adoption process in place. The social worker revisits the case, decides it is in the best interest of the child to reunite with the parent. The mother destroys the child's precious life! A little voice tragically silenced, in a cruel and heartless way. The end of the news report and the end of the innocent young life. Again, the heavy feeling in my chest and also my shoulders. The ache, the torture of reliving the question once again, the guilt of who dropped the ball?

The father of her son has made several police reports to more than one district in regard to Kya's whereabouts. He stops by my home.

He is very concerned because when he picks up his son, he remembers Kya would run and hide or peek out from behind a door. He recalls that, earlier, the mother was participating in classes with the county children's services. Lately, at his visits with his son, he has not seen Kya. He lately became concerned about his son's safety because the mother was frequently moving.

She told him of several incidents of violence. He became his son's caregiver, and his behavior improved also in school. The boy's father would inquire of Kya's whereabouts, and the mother said she was with various family members.

After coming to get his son, the mother confided in him that she wanted to be a better parent (schizophrenic). She made a mistake and hurt Kya when she was a baby. She stated that Kya was not coming back.

The boy's father called 696-kids and the police districts. The two police districts did not afford him the opportunity to even write a formal report. The authorities dismissed it as a custody issue and "*not a safety issue.*" He said the mother sent a text to him that she felt like "giving up." Police reports information: What are parents, family, and citizens to do?

Dear Journal,

There is no contact with Kya now! The mother lied. The paternal grandfather has knocked on doors at the given addresses, trying to trace our baby. No leads, and the neighborhood search is less than five miles away. The paternal grandparents continue to knock on doors and call with no answers from the misinformation by Children and Family Services.

I teach second grade at the nearby school. The kindergarten teacher says that she believes Kya was enrolled for the fall but never showed up. I am frantically searching.

Dear Journal,

The call was made to the clerk of courts office of the juvenile division. This suggestion was made by the news reporter. All the case records were willingly mailed to me (I paid the postage gladly) by an officer of the court. We communicated several times. There are over one hundred papers on file concerning the mother and her four children, the specific cases (after previously being told there were no records of Kya).

One of the papers revealed (after the fact) that the specific action steps were later changed quietly by the social worker. She amended the plan "goal" to (1) reflect the plan of reunification and (2) for visitation to gradually increase if all continued to *go well*.

What specifically does that mean? It's a big change to the previous plans, which I am not aware of. *Why?*

This is to acknowledge the clerk of courts. You took the time out of your busy schedule to "care" for a family in crisis and, very importantly, mailed the much-needed copies of the court documents. Thank you for following through. Your work is not completed in vain. *Thank you!* The written communication allows the legal loopholes to be openly explored.

Item 2 was for visitation to gradually increase if all continued to *go well*.

What is "go well"? It's too vague. Yes, it is going well for all. Why? Because Kya is placed in a loving home with her paternal grandmother. No. It is not easy or perfect, but she is safe and lovingly cared for. The child's basic needs plus some are being addressed and met at this time. Even the court review board agreed with this placement.

Something went *terribly* wrong. The decision was overruled.

Dear Journal,

The grandmother's permanency is to take place in November. The social worker plans to continue to monitor the case and terminate Children and Family Services in October.

However, the review of Structured Decision Making results one year earlier states, "Reunification is not the goal." The needs reassessment checked yes to call priority for mother. It lists preferred continued services for emotional stability, employment, and the need for stable housing.

That was why the family could not locate Kya. No one knew where she lived. Incorrect addresses were given to the agency. How do these interventions protect a child from immediate danger? The box check for placement is "Reunification is *not* the goal."

Dear Journal,

Yesterday was Kya's birthday. I am in her auntie's home. I am babysitting my other granddaughter, a puppy, and a guinea pig.

My writing has temporarily ceased because it is Kya's tenth-year heavenly birthday. My soul still aches. I dropped the ball. *So tragic.*

The feeling is deep depression. Pressure of a ten-year past forgotten by others No. I think of my granddaughter most often. Fond memories and reminders frame my actions and present thoughts. Now more information is being revealed, and more facts are provided by the courts.

My feelings are that child advocacy did not protect her but returned her in harm's way despite the review of the Structured Decision Making (SDM) results.

The results were that "reunification is *not* the goal." Notation being Children and Family Services included the need for "stable housing."

More time and effort continue to be put forth to research into what exactly happened before and after the occurrence of the missing child. Blame all involved for the terrible consequences.

Recent news!

Dear Journal,

Bones were recently found at a factory site. I cringed at the thought.

The phone rings, and it is a friend calling. "You sound so down, sad. What's the matter?"

I related to her the information I had just heard. My friend told me to take it easy. No worries. However, each time, there was news of finding bones in a landfill. Then came the curiosity and pain of finding out if Kya's remains had been uncovered.

No. It is not her!

Dear Journal,

The family and friends hold a candlelight vigil in front of the last known address. This is where the mother stated the fatal accident occurred. A piece of furniture fell on the child. The body was somehow placed into a trash bag and set out on the lawn.

The people form a circle, holding candles and balloons with Kya's name on them. The house is dark. I shake with tears as the mourners disperse. (My job/school is very close by.) Why?

Recent news!

Dear Journal,

The neighbor at the mother's house reports a trash bag on the lawn with bones in it. Is this the missing link? What happened? A lot of questions go through my head. My stomach aches, and my head hurts.

The police are called. The forensic report comes back that the bones are those of a dog. I am devastated and crash out on the couch. Help me, Lord!

There is a burning desire to know what exactly happened! Where is Kya? The uncertainty lingers. *Still, no body is found.* The hearsay conclusions are not enough to bring me closure.

Recent news

The historical moment in 1977 was a United States Supreme Court. In the Inez Joyce Moore case, the court ruled that a state zoning ordinance that prohibited a grandmother from living with her grandchildren was unconstitutional forty-five years ago. She took her battle to the Supreme Court. Grandparents' rights act to keep the structure of the Black family and all-American families. Grandparents are an intricate weave into the family pattern. Grandparents can play a strong part in family stability.

Dear Journal,

One family member and her children went school shopping. Kya was with her mother at the same store.

Kya was hiding behind the clothes racks and did not want to come out. She was afraid. Total introvert! It was reported that Kya looked terrified of her mother.

Everyone quickly left.

I truly wanted to be there where my granddaughter was last seen! Lord, help me!

Dear Journal,

My mind is burdened, consumed now of thoughts of my missing granddaughter. (Her mother said she put her in the trash.) Alone at my home, feeling rather tired, I go downstairs to my basement.

I look into the far left corner. There, I envision, are little children crouched down, hovering there together in a small group of about twelve. Mixed children of girls and boys, white and black. One little girl steps out of the group of children. I say, "Come here, Kya. Come to Grandmother." And she walks toward me.

This is the end of my *vision*. I cry in silence—the worst hurt. And I return up the stairs, alone with my thoughts.

Dear Journal,

The guilt is taking over my life. A few friends listen to my personal feelings when they call me. I consult with my pastor.

The first time I heard of Kya being put into the trash was through a news reporter. He called and asked to come to my home. I was lost, wandering mentally and physically, not knowing how to react to the tragic news. *No, not my family. Not my grandbaby.*

It was Sunday morning. I was in shock and total depression—in a *very dark place* surrounded by grief. I did not dress. I could not handle it, but I *walked* to the nearest church in my pj's with my jacket over it. I wore house shoes and did not comb hair. I sat in the far right corner of the pew, the last seat in the very back. I was invisible, or so I thought. The church service had already started. *Lord, help me.* Nothing to do. All used up, but I silently ask for help. I did not really hear the sermon but did feel some calming solace there.

I felt cold then very hot. Things were in a daze. The congregation probably assumed I was mentally ill or an addict. They all ignored me. I was sitting alone after the congregation left. I was not able to get up!

The pastor came, sat by me, and asked, "Do you need a pastor? I'll be your pastor."

I wanted to feel invisible. It felt better that way.

The pastor's understanding and sincere compassion gave me the strength to leave the church that horrific day. Weeks later, I returned to become an active member. Thank you, Lord.

Sometimes the tears fall down my cheeks at church service, and my spirit seems broken. *The people do not know my story!* Judge me not because I sing too loudly!

Dear Journal,

There is added confusion when the TV reporter returned to my home. He wanted a follow-up to this case.

I went to legal counseling. The lawyers refused to take the case. Lost, where do I go from here? Write a book.

I never got money or any type of reimbursement for supporting my granddaughter. I never asked for compensation, which was not an issue.

The blame for the tragedy of my granddaughter put in the trash can be shared. It is a universal dilemma. It is a horror that is recognized, but far too often, it is acknowledged and soon afterward overlooked and forgotten.

Again, the heavy feeling in my chest and now also in my shoulders. The ache, the torture of it all…but I must finish this book! Time to pause to walk the puppy in this beautiful fall-like weather. Nature's visuals: puffy white clouds and artistic pine trees under the blue skies.

This writing is to bring awareness and uncover one more tragic "drop the ball" case of child abuse and a child "put in the trash." The intended outcome is to initiate the discussion and reevaluation for the reforming of laws and promoting the enactment of laws granting custody rights to established grandparents where not recognized.

I am an educator and have worked for years with caseworkers and social workers, realizing that, all too often, the individual caseloads are heavy and the demands too time-consuming.

The follow-up case visits are crucial after the hearings are completed and decisions are made. The legal terms look very organized written down.

The parties involved were probably impressed at that time. The family feels committed to the planned program. Then reality sets in! If the caseworker stays in face-to-face contact. It is very important to see what the situation may really be.

Not assumptions. Not rose-colored glasses. The child may be returning to a volatile life-threatening situation. Pop-up visits. Door-to-door visits at least every two weeks. "Hello. I see you are okay. See you soon." This way, needed referrals or the child can perhaps be better serviced. This leads to closer, tighter interventions and follow-ups to follow through for the child's safety and whereabouts.

Semiannual board reviews are not enough. Action steps written on paper are not enough. If grandparents and family members are willing to assist, train them to be effective parts in the child's life.

Established grandparents may provide the stability, guidance, and love the child deserves.

Nobody's trash!

Dear Journal,

Now I am holding on to emptiness. The disturbed mother says she put my Kya in the trash. There is no trace of her, and nothing has been reported. No body has been uncovered. Therefore, there is no closure in the case of my granddaughter.

The social worker mailed Kya's journal from the courts: "A Book About Me." It is a green-and-black paperback book. Kya's name is written on the front along with her birthdate information.

It is noted to insert snapshots, school photos, birth certificate, handprint, and drawings into the book. The first pages of Kya's journal are instructions. The next pages are entitled "Names of My Birth Family." The blue page is sadly blank. However, the maternal grandmother's name is listed because she took Kya home from the hospital when she was born.

The next page of Kya's journal from the county is the social worker's explanation of "Why I Couldn't Live with My family," which is also sadly blank. The next page is labeled "Places I've Lived." There are three entries. The maternal grandmother, the foster mother, and the paternal grandmother (me).

That is where her little life dreams ended. The pink page words are "Where I Live Now." Sadly, there is no entry. It is blank. Then "Achievements." In the "first words" entry, I filled in *hot, bye, Nana, eat,* and SpongeBob ☺. Her first steps fourteen months, weaned fifteen months, toilet trained beginning at twenty months old. Nothing was filled in her journal before that time. Only the time we spent together.

"Memories of Places I've Lived" is a blank yellow page. "Schools I've Attended" is a blank blue page. No nursery school or notes up to grade 12 schooling. Nothing was filled in because her future was savagely destroyed.

The "Health" records were up-to-date. In "My Favorite Things to Do," I wrote that Kya liked to play with toys, the bike, the dollhouse, and the piano. Kya also tried to write and color books at eighteen months old. I took Kya for a dental checkup and recorded regular checkups with the pediatrician.

Most unfortunately, this ends Kya's short journal as well as her precious young life. Grandmother loves you! Expressing fond memories of you!

The very last journal topic was "Where I Live Now." It is very sad.

There is no closure. Rest in peace, precious.

My granddaughter has not been found! The tragic mystery sends aches and feelings of deep regret through the core of my very soul—a desperation for answers, for the ugly truth to be revealed. My eyes are feeling so heavy this minute, opening up to a very dark place. I will stop writing temporarily.

The news reporter who visited my home asked the question, "Are there any suggestions towards the awareness to help other children lost in the system?" The news reporter also offered to assist in upholding the life legacy of Kya.

There were breakdowns in communication that are being found to be major destructive factors. The motion to terminate protective services has been filed by Children and Family Services. The motion was filed and approved through the mother's private legal counsel. The letters were sent out to all parties involved in the initial *hearings* with the exception of the paternal grandmother, who could have interrupted the immediate reunification decision because it was out of order as to prior hearings.

The petition filed by the court to adopt and the classes taken by the paternal grandmother were completely ignored. The paternal grandmother would have interrupted the immediate reunification decision. Probably, it's why I did not receive a letter to inform me. Why wasn't the paternal grandmother present at this important hearing?

After all, she is the current caregiver and has a petition for adoption. The County prosecutor has copies of all the other parties present, names and requests. *But not mine!* By my not being in court, it was easier to overturn the petition.

The mother's legal counsel simply ignored it. The court was looking through "rose-colored glasses" or (one could say) taking the easy way out. Closing the case—one and done. Remember, the social worker has plans for an out-of-state full wedding next month. After that, the case would pass down to another social worker to be continued. *That did not happen.* Overload?

This crucial decision was made to reunify child with mother also at a *semiannual review filing.* The decision was made far too quickly without consideration of *all* the parties' *best interests,* regardless of the parties' status previously established. That was wrong! Especially because the review team initially recommended continued custody and placement filings of specific action steps.

This is the process presented in this case only. The specific evidence and procedures for only this particular case. Needless to say, the details of others are not known, or they may or may not be similar cases. If it is similar, it is *purely coincidental.* This does not, in any way, relate to the author's personal viewpoint expressed in this book.

All names and places have been changed to protect the innocent and the not-so-innocent, the guilty and the not guilty, the sane and the insane.

Everybody is somebody to somebody. We are loved. We are God's children. The little souls are precious and should be protected at all times. We are made differently but possess souls and spirits. This is the story of a lost little person with a big heart who only wanted to be loved and accepted. She is precious in God's sight.

Treat others as *you* would like to be treated, no matter the size, color, or age. We often speak of bullies in schools. Parents can also be bullies of the little precious cargo entrusted to them for various reasons and situations. They often forget that someone nurtured and raised us all. Someone put up with our inadequacies and saw to our needs. Stop children being illegally trashed!

Remember your personal struggles, your anxieties, your issues, your fears growing up. Fears of the dark, of the cellar, of animals, of bullies, and of some grown-ups. Life is a gift, and if it becomes too much for you to handle, stop! Do not trash children. Share your miracle of life (child) with others who desire to love.

I love the Lord!

Recent news

Mother drove the car into the lake with two young children inside.

The family unit may resemble the shape of a pyramid. Social worker, mother, grandparents—these are the corners. The sides of the pyramid may represent life's twists and turns. The supports are the essential parts to the mother's health decisions. Children and Family Services did not connect the missing links of communication. The family failed to initiate the permanent bond and love. Grandparents definitely fit into the title of Children and Family Services

The reader may unwrap the book title. That is why it's the form of a Venn diagram.

The title may be expressed as one word or two or three words in any combination of words. It can also be expressed backward or forward. The intricate title draws conclusions to the important ending. The title draws conclusions from the details left to the reader's interpretation. Throughout the legal process, the crimes or mistakes are overlooked. The cycle leads to the horrific, tragic ending.

About the Author

Cora Fleeta Hill is a mother and a journal keeper of her incarcerated son. This is more than a life story because of all the pains of emotional, physical, and mental pressure involved. She works as an inner-city primary and preschool teacher. She earned a bachelor's degree in education K-8 at Adrian College in Adrian, Michigan. She received a master's degree in education K-8 from Cambridge College in Boston, Massachusetts, in the year 2002. Her form of relaxation is through acrylic scenery painting on canvas. Her favorite passion is music and playing the piano, and she often gives free piano lessons to children, which she loves. Cora also served as a Girl Scout leader and a Boy Scout den mother.

Her zodiac sign is Aquarius. She loves the Lord and attends Aldersgate United Methodist Church. She is a proud member of the Delta Sigma Theta Sorority Incorporated Alumnae Chapter. Cora has two children—one son and a daughter.

Amber Hill, the editor of this book, is Cora's daughter. Her zodiac sign is Libra. She earned a bachelor of science in nursing degree from the University of Akron in Ohio. She is the proud mother of two daughters: Dasj'a and D'Naya. Amber served as an essential nurse worker in Las Vegas, Nevada, during the coronavirus epidemic.

www.ingramcontent.com/pod-product-compliance
Lightning Source LLC
Chambersburg PA
CBHW022100150726
47990CB00003B/1177